PUSHING
THE BOUNDARIES

PEARSON

Prentice Hall

Boston, Massachusetts
Upper Saddle River, New Jersey

ISBN 0-13-363638-0

2 3 4 5 6 7 8 9 10   11 10 09 08

PRENTICE HALL DISCOVERIES

Pushing the Boundaries

What is the best way to communicate?

Table of Contents

THE SAMURAI
OF FEUDAL JAPAN

• • • • • • • • • •

Feudalism was a social system that existed in Japan from the 12th through the 19th centuries. The system, in which vassals provided military service to wealthy lords in exchange for land, gave Japan its social stability. It may be argued that the success of Japan's long-lasting feudal age can be attributed to two things. The first was the fact that Japan is an island nation, **isolated** from much of the world. The second was the "lord and vassal" relationship between the rich landholder, or *daimyo,* and the men of the warring class, the *samurai.*

A Samurai in Full

It is the year 1265 in Kamakura, Japan. A **brawny** *man
waits outside a door. His hair, knotted in a ponytail at the
front of his head, falls to the left, like a thick black tassel.
He wears a* hitatare, *a loose two-piece outfit that allows him
freedom of movement in battle. Its somber green color draws
little attention. The man bears a circular crest on his chest,
intricately woven with silk threads. It is his clan's crest, a mark
of pride. A black cloth belt is tied in front. From it hangs his*
daito *(long sword) and* shoto *(short sword). Like all members
of the warrior class, he wears his swords sheathed. Their han-
dles extend to his chest—within easy reach. He is a samurai.*

*The door opens. A young woman in a white kimono
bows her head then leads him to an inner room. There before
him, on a mat upon the floor, sits a portly man. He wears a
silvery-silk robe. He is a* daimyo *and the samurai's lord.*

*During this visit, the two men may speak of several things.
They may speak of the daimyo's farms, which the samurai
oversees. They may discuss the samurai's farm, which the
daimyo gave to him for his services. They may review the
defenses of the daimyo's land, which the samurai's army*
protects. *Or possibly, they will plan an attack on another
clan. They speak freely,* **uttering** *words without pretense or
lies. Such is the trust between the samurai and his lord.*

VOCABULARY

isolated (EYE suh layt uhd) *adj.* set apart

brawny (BRAWN ee) *adj.* strong and muscular

protects (proh TEKTS) *v.* shields from injury, danger, or loss;
guards; defends

utter (UT er) *v.* speak

A Code of Honor

By the year 1265, the relationship between samurai and daimyo had become the backbone of Japan's feudal society. The daimyos owned the land; the samurai protected it. The daimyos rewarded the samurais for their services. In return, the samurai pledged a **profound** loyalty to the daimyo's needs and wishes. His loyalty was a matter of honor.

The samurai code of honor—the "Way of the Warrior"—was similar to the European code of chivalry. Among other obligations, the code required the warrior to refuse surrender in battle and to die bravely in service to his lord. "Death is lighter than a feather," went the old saying, "but duty is weightier than a mountain." His bravery and skill in battle were a matter of pride to the samurai and his clan.

The military strength and moral integrity for which the samurai stood came to **represent** Japan's highest ideals. Some **conclude** it was these ideals that caused the beautiful arts and literature of feudal Japan to flourish.

The Origins of Japanese Feudalism

In the third century B.C., invaders from the Korean peninsula settled in Japan. They **transformed** Japan's Stone Age culture into an agricultural society.

Five hundred years later, around 200 A.D., China invaded the islands. It used its **considerable** military might to make Japan a tribute state of China. The Chinese brought much to Japan's culture, including the philosophy of Buddhism and a new writing system. Nevertheless, over the next several centuries, Japan would **strive** for independence. It created its own ruling class. It even had its own emperor, but the nation remained subservient to China.

By the end of the ninth century, China's ruling class began to decline. It lost its hold on the island nation. At long last, Japan was free.

VOCABULARY

profound (proh FOWND) *adj.* deeply or intensely felt

represent (REP ri ZENT) *v.* speak on behalf of someone; be a symbol that stands for something

conclude (kuhn KLOOD) *v.* form an opinion based on evidence

transform (trans FOHRM) *v.* change the shape or structure of something or someone

considerable (kuhn SID er uh buhl) *adj.* large enough to be important; worth noting

strive (STRYV) *v.* struggle; work hard

During the siege of Osaka castle, 400,000 samurai fought in a battle to the death.

The Rise of Japanese Feudalism

In the tenth and eleventh centuries, Japan's ruling class prospered and grew powerful. The power of the Japanese emperor rose to its peak. But challenges to that power were also rising.

Because ordinary Japanese shared little of Japan's wealth, many **loathed** the royal court and its wealthy ruling class. They **reacted** violently with rebellion. Meanwhile, warrior clans in the countryside were growing stronger. These warriors attached themselves to ruling families who could afford private armies. With the aid of the warriors, the ruling class could keep the rest of the population in line. In time, private armies, now called samurai, **enriched** their masters by seizing land and power from other clans.

One of these conflicts, between the Minamoto and the Taira clans, took place in 1259. It became one of the most important conflicts in Japanese history.

This painting shows Go-Toba, Japanese emperor from 1183 to 1198. He was placed on the throne by the Minamoto clan.

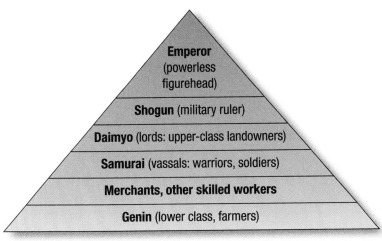

The Class Structure of Feudal Japan

The Minamoto and the Taira, two of the most powerful clans of Japanese aristocracy, fought each other for the total control of Japan. Ultimately, the Minamoto clan, backed by the samurai, won. The leader of the Minamoto appointed himself *shogun,* or military leader of Japan. An elite army of samurai supported his claim and enforced his laws. The emperor, though still revered, became powerless. Now, the shogun ruled Japan by the might of the sword.

The daimyos, the samurai warriors, the merchants and artisans, the farmers, in that order, lived under the shogun's authority. Thus was **established** the class hierarchy of feudal Japan. It would remain basically unchanged for 800 years.

Vocabulary

loathed (LOHTHD) *v.* hated

react (ree AKT) *v.* behave in a particular way in response to someone or something

enrich (en RICH) *v.* give more value or effectiveness to

establish (uh STAB lish) *v.* determine; make sure of; set up

An Enduring Society

Class System A feature common to all feudalistic societies is a class system in which every man, woman, and child has his or her place on the social ladder. A person rarely moves up or down this ladder. The children of peasants grow up to be peasants. The children of the ruling class grow up to be lords and ladies. This absence of social mobility discourages social change. Therefore, society tends to remain the same. This was one reason Japan's feudal system lasted so long. There were other reasons as well.

Geography Japan's geography helped to sustain its feudalistic society. Blessed with a mild climate, Japan flourished as an agricultural nation. Its soil, enriched by millennia of volcanic eruptions, provided fertile farmland that could feed the people. Japan's mountainous terrain, on the other hand, protected regional clans against invasion. Cross-mountain invasions could prove dangerous.

Isolation The fact that Japan is an island nation was of no small **benefit** to the feudalistic society. Being separated by sea from its nearest neighbors gave Japan advantage over would-be invaders. The sea also acted as a buffer between outside influences and Japanese culture. As a result, Japan nourished its own culture in splendid isolation. It didn't know what the rest of the world was doing, and it really didn't care.

Another factor that strengthened Japan's feudal society was its belief that God favored the nation. Of course, the power structure in Japan drew immense strength from the samurai. By 1100, the warrior class had already become indispensable in clan warfare. But could the samurai protect the land from aggressive outside nations?

VOCABULARY

benefit (BEN uh fit) *n.* a gain or positive result

This woodblock print shows Mount Haruna covered in snow. Mount Haruna is a volcanic mountain on the Japanese island of Honshu.

The Mongol Invasions

The test came in 1274 when Mongolian emperor Kublai Khan invaded Japan with an army of over 20,000 men. After a lengthy siege, the samurai did turn back the enemy. However, in 1281 Kublai Khan returned with the greatest fleet the world had ever seen: 4,000 ships carrying 150,000 men. On Japan's southern island of Kyushu, the Mongolians **engaged** the samurai in a seven-week battle. Then, quite suddenly, a typhoon **occurred**, which nearly destroyed the Mongol fleet.

This fictional **passage** captures the emotional impact of the event:

A Divine Wind *As the storm thrashed the shoreline, we huddled with our swords in huts atop the hill. The horses neighed; the wind whipped the thatch. There was a hole in the roof of our hut, and rain had soaked our sleeping mats. Outside, the drinking-water barrels over-flowed. The air smelled of wet clothes and mud.*

Kublai Khan is shown giving his golden seal to Marco Polo. Kublai Khan tried to invade Japan twice, but failed both times.

Day became night. We could not see the Mongol ships anchored along the shore below. We could not see the enemy's tents along the beach. For more than seven weeks, we had set upon our foe, blood for blood. But today the battle belonged to the storm.

VOCABULARY

engaged (en GAYJD) *v.* entered into conflict with
occur (uh KER) *v.* happen; take place
passage (PAS ij) *n.* a section of writing

Soon the morning crept upon us, clear and quiet. As the sun rose, I stepped out of our hut alone and looked down upon the shore.

Where tents had stood, I saw seaweed and timbers. Where foreign flags had flown, seabirds circled. Just off the beach, where the ships of a foe had made anchor, a gentle breeze raised a mist off a **luminous** *sea.*

I stood mute, doubting my eyes. A divine wind had swept our enemies back into the sea! We had not raised a sword, nor fired an arrow—but in one raging night, scores of invaders had been **expelled**.

The Mongol invasion of 1281 was the largest enemy threat in Japan's history. The Japanese were hopelessly outnumbered. Defeat seemed inevitable. Yet they emerged victorious because a "divine wind" greatly reduced the number of the enemy. Many Japanese viewed the epic typhoon as proof that God favored their nation. They also concluded that the samurai were the world's greatest warriors. They believed, in short, that God and samurai had made Japan invincible.

Vocabulary

luminous (LOO muh nuhs) *adj.* giving off light
expel (ex SPEL) *v.* drive out by force; eject; dismiss

A typhoon with high waves destroyed Kublai Khan's fleet.

The Decline of the Samurai

Contrary to the normal way of the class system, the samurai did climb the social ladder, moving from rough warrior clans to a ruling military class. Once they reached this high rung it seemed they were there to stay. As long as there was plenty of warrior work to be done, the samurai's high place in the social order seemed guaranteed.

Constant warfare **generated** plenty of work for the samurai. Fierce battles between hostile clans and warlords were frequent and fierce. During the late 15th century, however, things began to change.

After a hundred years of civil war, the ruling shogun lost control of the country. Another powerful samurai, Toyotomi Hideyoshi, took over the government.

Under Hideyoshi's rule, life changed for the samurai. Hideyoshi ordered them to live in castles, away from their personal land. Until that time, samurai warriors farmed their own land during peacetime. The purpose for this measure was part of a larger plan. Hideyoshi wanted to create a **distinct** separation between the classes. Warriors were strictly separated from farmers. Lords were strictly separated from warriors. The merchant class was strictly separated from the ruling class.

Because samurai could no longer farm their lands, they had to rely on a government tax for their peacetime livelihood. Fortunately for them, the country was continually wracked by wars.

Vocabulary

generate (JEN er ayt) *v.* produce or create something
distinct (dis TINGKT) *adj.* separate and different

16

Toyotami Hideyoshi is shown here blowing a conch shell.
Hideyoshi ruled Japan in the late 1500s.

Emperor Meiji ruled Japan from 1867 to 1912. By the time of his death, Japan had undergone great changes. Japan became known as one of the great powers in the world.

Then, from the 17th through the 18th centuries, a powerful samurai clan brought peace to the land. This **affected** the samurai greatly. Peace did not favor the warrior class. It left them with nothing to do. Many samurai were dismissed from their lord's employ. Some became bureaucrats, or found other forms of employment. Some just wandered the land looking for work. Some became outlaws. Many, though, lived a life of idle wealth and privilege. The samurai was still the elite class in a feudal state. But that, too, was about to change.

The End of the Feudal State

In 1869 the last shogun stepped aside. Once more, an emperor ruled Japan. The new ruler, Emperor Meiji, was a forward thinker. He could hear the western world, with its new technologies and modern ideas, knocking at the door. Meiji was determined to end Japan's isolationism. He wanted to establish a modern nation. In his new Japan, there would be no class distinction. To **achieve** this end, he ordered the daimyo to return their lands to the emperor. He made the samurai give up their privileges—and their swords. In 1871 he officially abolished the feudal system and the samurai class.

Vocabulary

affect (uh FEKT) *v.* produce a change in or have an influence over something or someone

achieve (uh CHEEV) *v.* succeed in doing something; accomplish; gain

19

The Last Samurai

The samurai warrior was intrinsically tied to the feudal world in which he lived. When that world ended, the samurai no longer had a purpose. He had to go, but, in true samurai fashion, he did not go without a fight.

In 1877, an army of samurai warriors went to war against Japan's new army. The new army was trained in modern warfare. It was swords against guns. The samurai fought bravely through several battles, but they knew their effort was futile. On the morning of September 24, 1877, the last band of warriors rode into battle with drawn swords. The government army cut them down with artillery. In samurai tradition, the leader committed suicide and the last warriors standing beheaded each other. The days of the samurai were over.

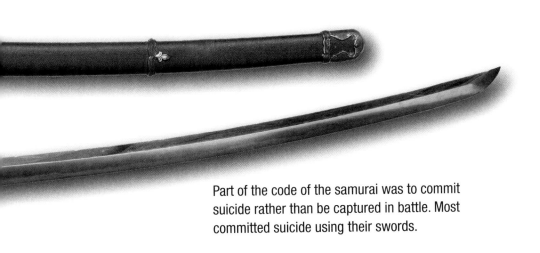

Part of the code of the samurai was to commit suicide rather than be captured in battle. Most committed suicide using their swords.

Discussion Questions

1. Today in Japan, the samurai is glorified as a national hero. Considering the samurai's role in his society, do you think this glorification is justified? Why or why not?

2. How did the daimyo and the samurai both benefit by their relationship? Name some similar relationships in modern society and tell how they benefit each other.

3. Societies are constantly changing. When they do, some things are lost or left behind. Name some ways in which our society is changing. Discuss how these changes affect our jobs, our cultural behaviors, and our ways of life. What will be lost or left behind?

VOLCANOES
EARTH'S FIERY BREATH

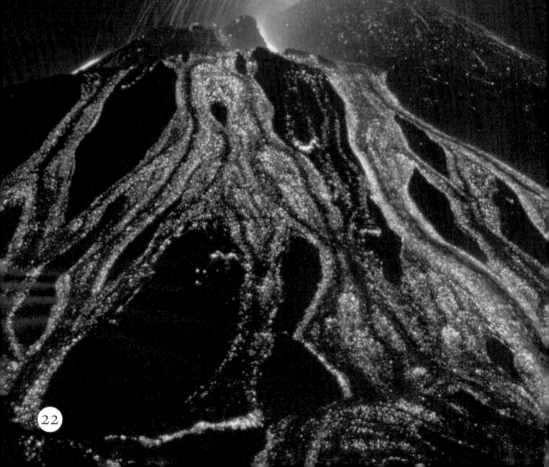

January 14, 1993: It was 1:00 P.M. in Colombia, near the Ecuador border. Hot gases rose from the crater of Galeras Volcano. Orange pools of molten rock bubbled inside.

"Six of us were working on the rim of the crater," Professor Stanley Williams recalls. Six other vulcanologists had descended *into* the volcano. Two of them were collecting a sample of sulfurous gases three times hotter than the planet Mercury.

By 1:43 P.M., several **curious** tourists and journalists stood **transfixed** to the spot, observing this otherworldly scene. Suddenly, rocks **dislodged** from the crater walls. Then "before anyone [could] react," Williams says, "the first explosion blew large blocks at such high speeds . . . that all those in the crater or on the rim (except me) were killed." The vulcanologists' worst nightmare had been realized.

VOCABULARY

curious (KYOOR ee uhs) *adj.* eager to learn or know
transfixed (tranz FIKST) *adj.* rooted to or focused on a spot
dislodge (dis LAHJ) *v.* force from a position or place

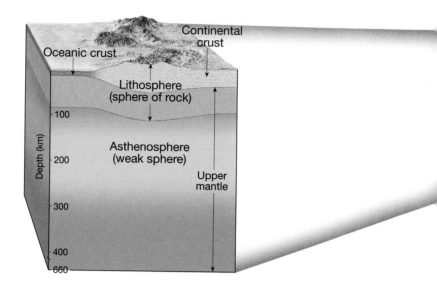

The Making of a Volcano

A volcanic eruption can be one of the most terrifying forces on Earth. It is also one of the most fascinating. The *making* of a volcano is equally so.

A volcano is a hill or mountain made from *pyroclastic* material and lava. Rock fragments, ash, and gases make up pyroclastic materials. Lava is basically *magma* or molten rock that quickly hardens as it cools. Magma and pyroclastic materials erupt from Earth's interior.

No one knows with certainty what lies beneath Earth's surface. Geologists do **infer**, however, that Earth has four-layers **consisting** of the crust, the mantle, the core, and the inner core.

Magma originates in the upper mantle or lower crust. It usually escapes at the seams between the *tectonic* plates of Earth's crust. When these plates shift and grind

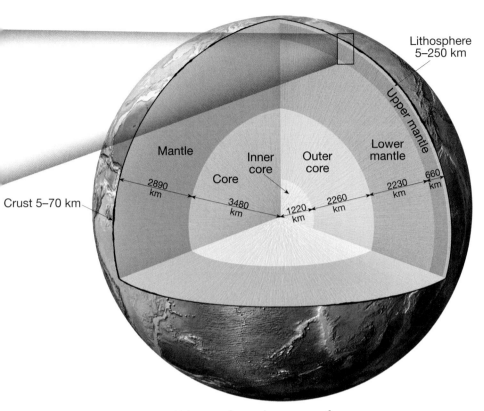

Volcanoes form when magma from
Earth's mantle reaches Earth's surface.

against each other they can cause earthquakes. They
can also force magma and other materials up through
the seams, or the *plate boundaries,* to Earth's surface.

Over time, a buildup of hardened lava and pyroclastic
materials forms the volcanic mountain.

VOCABULARY

infer (in FER) *v.* make a logical assumption based on evidence
or reasoning

consist (kuhn SIST) *v.* to be made of

Sicily's Mount Etna is Europe's tallest active volcano.
It is nearly 11,000 feet high.

Mountains of the Gods

Many ancient cultures deify volcanoes. Ancient Greeks
saw volcanic mountains as the domain of Hephaestus,
the god of fire. The word *volcano* comes from the name
Vulcan, the Roman god of fire. Hawaii honors Pele as
the fire goddess. Northwest Indians have the god Loowit.
The list is long.

   Unfortunately, the gods can be cruel. In 1963 on the
Indonesian island of Bali, the islanders gathered for a
special ceremony. This same ceremony took place every
hundred years in temples on Mount Agung. This time,
the festival had an added feature.

   Agung, a volcano long asleep, **displayed** signs of
awakening. It began to tremble. Small lava flows streamed

from the crater's walls. The island worshipers stood enrapt in spiritual awe. Thousands flocked to the slopes. Then, in 1964, Mount Agung erupted. In minutes, hot ash and deadly gas killed over a thousand people.

This terrible tragedy, though not the deadliest among volcanic eruptions, might have been prevented had the islanders received sufficient warning.

THE SEVEN DEADLIEST VOLCANOES IN RECORDED HISTORY			
Volcano (Type) Location, Year	Total Deaths	Major Causes of Deaths	Environmental Effects
Tambora (Composite) Indonesia, 1815	70,000– 92,000	starvation, pyroclastic flows	Ash and gas reach stratosphere; global cooling, crops fail in Europe.
Krakatau (Composite) Indonesia, 1883	36,000– 40,000	tsunamis	Much of volcano and island fall into the sea, setting off 120-foot waves that smash nearby islands.
Mont Pelée (Dome) Martinique, 1902	30,000	pyroclastic flows	Burns city of St. Pierre; kills everyone except one jailed prisoner.
Nevado del Ruiz (Composite) Colombia, 1985	23,000	lahars (ash and debris)	Buries the town of Amero; devastates farmland and deluges rivers.
Unzen (Composite) Japan, 1792	15,000	pyroclastic flow, landslide; tsunami	Explosion of ash and debris ruins the city of Shimabara; tsunamis in turn wrack the coast.
Vesuvius (Composite) Italy, 79 AD and 1631	5,000 3,500 (1631)	pyroclastic flows	Lava and pyroclastic flows leave gruesome trails in Pompeii (79 AD) and in Torre del Greco (1631).
Mt. Pinatubo (Composite) Philippines, 1991	700	pyroclastic flows	Property destroyed, land turned barren; gases in atmosphere lower world temperatures by 5°F.

VOCABULARY

display (di SPLAY) *v.* exhibit objects and feelings so they can be seen easily

While ancient cultures have deified volcanoes, modern science has demystified them. Vulcanologists, **challenged** by fiery craters and molten lava, pursue their research into the very mouth of fire. In learning about volcanic formations and activity, vulcanologists find better ways to **detect** early signs of eruptions.

Types of Volcanoes

Not all volcanoes are created equal. Basically, there are four types: cinder cones, lava domes, shield volcanoes, and composite volcanoes.

Cinder Cones

Cinder cones are the simplest and smallest volcano type. They consist of cinders, hard lava, and basaltic fragments ejected from a single vent. Basalt is a dark rock rich in iron and magnesium.

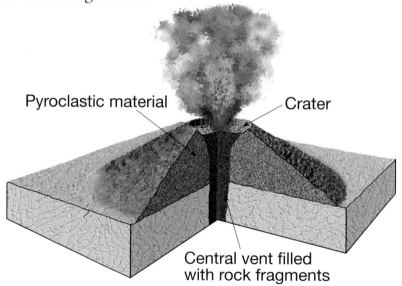

Pyroclastic material   Crater

Central vent filled with rock fragments

Explosive eruptions from cinder cone volcanoes throw lava high into the air. As the cooled lava falls, it forms steep slopes.

Cinders range mostly from olive-sized to softball-sized chunks. With their cragginess and bubble-cavities, they look like black or red sea sponge. The chunks form a steep cone-shaped mound, with a small crater at the top. Usually cinder cones appear in clusters.

This picture shows a cinder cone north of Flagstaff, Arizona.

One of nature's best volcanic shows **occurs** when a cinder cone erupts at night. It can shoot sprays of red lava high into the night sky. Yet the eruptions are small enough to safely watch the **luminous** fireworks from close by.

On February 20, 1943, a rare spectacle unfolded. A fissure in a cornfield opened. Ash and lava shot out and a new cinder cone began to grow. The world watched in fascination, but a farmer named Dionisio Pulido had the best view. It happened on his farm, near Parícutin, Mexico.

"The ground swelled," Pulido explained, "and raised itself seven or eight feet high. . . . [A] kind of smoke or fine dust . . . began to rise from part of the crack. . . . [M]ore smoke billowed out, with a hiss or whistle. . . . And there was a smell of sulfur."

Vocabulary

challenge (CHAL uhnj) *v.* call to take part in a contest or competition

detect (dee TEKT) *v.* notice or discover something

occur (uh KER) *v.* happen; take place

luminous (LOO muh nuhs) *adj.* giving off light

By next day, the mound had reached 35 feet and rocks were flying out of it. The volcano, now named Parícutin, erupted **incessantly** for 9 years, ejecting 1.7 billion cubic meters of ash and lava. By 1952, a cinder cone 1400 feet tall loomed over Pulido's now-barren field.

Lava Domes

Lava dome volcanoes form from bulbous masses of hot syrupy lava. This thick lava travels slowly and only short distances. So as it erupts, the viscous lava piles over and around the vent. It then hardens to leave a big plug, or dome, over the vent.

Volcanic domes usually form in the crater or on the slope of large composite volcanoes. A lava dome has been forming in the crater of Mount St. Helens since its eruption in 1980.

Mont Pelée Blows Its Top Lava domes usually pose less danger than open-crater volcanoes. Mont Pelée is an exception. This is partly a coincidence of geography. The city of St. Pierre sits at Pelée's foot, on the coast of the Caribbean island of Martinique.

Gases and lava expand domes from within, and sometimes pressure and thrust explode these thick plugs. On May 8, 1902, Mont Pelée blew its top and loosed a hot volcanic hurricane. Before Pelée erupted, explosions and sulfurous smells had loomed for two months. Yet, sadly, authorities failed to **communicate** the danger. No one was evacuated. The pyroclastic flow killed nearly 30,000 people in the city of St. Pierre.

Pelée was the deadliest volcano of the twentieth century.

Shield Volcanoes

Like cinder cones and lava domes, shield volcanoes take their name from their shape. The photograph of Mauna Loa shows how its broad gentle slopes look something like a warrior's shield.

Shield volcanoes are constructed from fluid lava flows. Out of underground reservoirs basaltic magma rises through a central vent or group of vents. As it slowly streams away from the crater, the lava hardens into gradual slopes or plateaus. Lava may also erupt from fractures on the cone's flanks.

Some of the world's largest volcanoes are shields. One of these goliaths is Mauna Loa.

Vocabulary

incessantly (in SES uhnt lee) *adv.* without stopping

communicate (kuh MYOO ni kayt) *v.* to make ideas or feelings known

Quiet eruptions spread out lava in flat layers.
The lava builds a gentle slope when it cools. This
creates shield volcanoes, such as Mauna Loa.

Mauna Loa, a Gentle Giant Mauna Loa is the largest volcano on our planet. For ages, lava has flowed from Mauna Loa. The entire "big island" of Hawaii was actually formed from the melding of Mauna Loa and four other volcanoes. They rank among the most active volcanoes in the world. Among them is fiery Kilauea, the domain of the goddess Pele.

Hawaii, in fact, is a series of shield volcanoes that sprang from the ocean floor. Hawaii doesn't sit over a plate boundary, however. It sits above a "hot-spot."

Way out, under the Pacific Ocean floor, a giant magma pipe, a "hot spot," has been gushing torrents of lava for 70 million years. As lava pumps into the cold water, it forms into rock. A lot of rock. Enough to rise from the ocean floor and form the Hawaiian Islands.

Native Hawaiians love their volcanoes. They love their volcanic fireworks and impressive lava flow. Yet the natives have learned to live with these dangerous mountains by keeping a respectful distance.

Composite Volcanoes

Composite volcanoes rank among Earth's grandest mountains. Mount Fuji in Japan and Mount Rainier in Washington State are among them. Vulcanologist Richard V. Fisher describes composite volcanoes as "graceful solitary cones." They can soar 10,000 feet above their bases.

They often stand alone, miles apart. Yet viewed from on high, they sit in long chains. For instance, the Pacific Ocean's Ring of Fire stretches thousands of miles.

Such volcanic chains occur along seams between Earth's giant tectonic plates.

Composite volcanoes are made from layers of rubble deposited over long periods of time. Lava, volcanic ash, cinders, and blocks form the alternate layers.

Most composite volcanoes have a crater at the summit. Within it runs a central vent or a cluster of vents. Lava flows out of breaks in the crater wall or from fissures leading out to the slopes. As lava hardens in these long cracks, it **reinforces** the cone.

This structure gives composite volcanoes strength to attain great height. However, the framework *can* crack.

Vocabulary

reinforce (REE in FOHRS) *v.* make stronger; support

Eruptions of composite volcanoes vary between quiet and violent. This forms layers in the volcano.

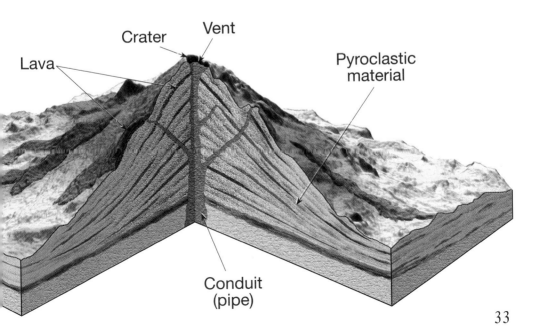

33

Mount St. Helens Awakes After a 123-year rest, Mount St. Helens in Washington State was about to awake with a bang.

As with most composite volcanoes, a plate boundary runs under Mount St. Helens. On March 20, 1980, an earthquake revealed a **considerable** amount of tectonic action beneath the mountain. Far below the moving plates, magma was rising.

On March 27, Mount St. Helens awoke. An explosion opened a 250-foot crater in its peak. A bulge began to grow on the north face. The bulge grew five feet per day, like a huge stone tumor. Small earthquakes continued to occur daily.

Tourists came to watch small explosions issue from the volcano's peak. They watched black ash cover the mountain's snowy slopes. They watched as the crater widened

to 1,500 feet. The once beautiful Mount St. Helens now looked sinister.

Mount St. Helen's Explodes On April 3, geologists detected magma deep in the volcano's cone. The chance to see a real eruption attracted even more people from far and wide. Their **attitude** was festive. Vendors sold tee shirts and hot dogs.

Vocabulary

considerable (kuhn SID er uh buhl) *adj.* large enough to be important; worth noting

attitude (AT uh tood) *n.* opinions or feelings, positive or negative, about something or someone

Mount St. Helens erupted violently on May 18, 1980.

At 8:32 A.M. on May 18, the people got their show: The stone tumor burst. The north side of the volcano collapsed dramatically. Then Mount St. Helens burst forth with a truly epic blast! Suddenly, the festive atmosphere turned tragic.

A volcanic ash cloud mushroomed into the sky like an atomic bomb! Cubic tons of *tephra,* a mix of volcanic rock and glass, spewed forth. A hot black cloud billowed off the summit. Tourists and local residents ran for their lives.

So much ash spewed skyward that it turned day to night. Meanwhile, glaciers melted on Mount St. Helens' peak and caused a *lahar,* a **torrent** of water and pyroclastic debris. In just hours, the lahar dropped millions of cubic yards of volcanic mud into the valley. It clogged the rivers and reservoirs. And that was just the beginning.

The landscape was totally **transformed**. Lava, 1300°F, ran 120 feet deep in some places. Mudslides covered 27 square miles. Four billion board feet of trees were flattened. Twenty-seven bridges and 200 homes were blown apart, buried, or swept away.

Almost 200 miles of roads were destroyed. No one can even calculate the loss of wildlife.

Most tragically, 57 people lost their lives. Luckily, vulcanologists working through government agencies had communicated the impending danger to everyone in the area. Most people **cooperated** with the enforced evacuation plan. If not, the loss of human life could have been far worse.

VOCABULARY

torrent (TOHR uhnt) *n.* flood; rush

transform (trans FOHRM) *v.* change the shape or structure of something or someone

cooperate (koh AHP er AYT) *v.* work together with others for a common purpose

The eruption of Mount St. Helens blew down an entire forest. Photographers explored the ash-covered forest after the eruption.

The Power of Volcanoes

Yes, volcanoes can be deadly, but they **benefit** Earth as well. Volcanic eruptions distribute minerals that enrich Earth's soil. Lava flows create islands. Volcanic steam, condensed over millions of years, formed the oceans, lakes, and rivers that give our planet life.

Humankind has always respected and **appreciated** the power of volcanoes. The number of ancient volcano gods

Mt. Pelée is a cinder cone volcano on the island of Martinique in the French West Indies. It is famous for the May 8, 1902 eruption that killed 29,000 people and destroyed the city of St. Pierre.

proves this. Today, we still stand in awe before volcanic mountains even when they are sleeping. Because humankind has no control over their awesome force, it has learned to watch and be wary.

We also appreciate the importance of volcano science. Vulcanology has **contributed** knowledge to grand subjects: the origin of continents, the structure of our planet. By predicting impending eruptions, it has also saved thousands of lives.

Whether we love them or fear them, volcanoes will always captivate us with the power of Earth's fiery breath.

Discussion Questions

1. What do you think motivates vulcanologists in their **risky** pursuit of research? Consider the events on Galeras Volcano in Colombia in 1993.

2. What do volcanoes, like other forces of nature such as hurricanes and earthquakes, teach us about humankind and its relationship to the natural world?

3. Even though scientists have done much to demystify volcanoes, our ancient desire to deify them remains. Why is this so?

VOCABULARY

benefit (BEN uh fit) *v.* give or receive help

appreciate (uh PREE shee AYT) *v.* be grateful for; recognize worth of something or someone

contribute (kuhn TRIB yoot) *v.* give or share money, knowledge, or ideas

risky (ris KEE) *adj.* hazardous; dangerous

ARCHITECTURE
and Changing Ideas of Shape, Form, and Beauty

by Deanne W. Kells

Downtown Boston, Massachusetts, has a mixture of old and new architecture.

Sometimes when you're inside a public building, you barely notice the structure around you. You go about your business. You feel safe and secure. At other times, a building can take your breath away with its beauty or amazing features. Both types of responses show that a building's architect has been successful. Any well-designed building has three basic characteristics, first identified by the Roman architect Vitruvius more than 2,000 years ago. First, a building must suit its purpose or function. Second, a building must last through time and be safe. Third, a building must delight the people it serves— whether that comes through a building's beauty or because it is so perfect for its use.

Through the ages, ideas about beauty have changed and different types of buildings have become necessary in the world. Architects have responded with intelligence and creativity. By studying great public buildings through time, we can notice big changes and understand why they occurred.

The Beginnings of Western Architecture

Scholars have argued about when Western architecture began. However, many people agree that ancient Greece and Rome **represent** the beginnings of a grand tradition. That is, what we can see in architecture from these two great civilizations we can still see in architecture today. Additionally, classical Greek architecture represented a **distinct** new style when it blossomed around the eighth century B.C.E.

This style arose to meet a new desire among the people to create temples that looked different from other buildings. Temples were where the people went to honor their gods and goddesses. The Greeks decided that temples should be big. Temples should **impress** people with their perfect proportions and simple yet graceful shapes.

The Parthenon The most famous of the ancient Greek temples is the Parthenon. The Parthenon stood on the highest hill of Athens. As people reached the top of the steps and entered the gate, they were looking at a corner and two sides of the temple. Right away they could see its grand size and perfect dimensions. These were marks of beauty that any Greek would **appreciate**.

The Parthenon was made entirely of marble. Tall columns marched all the way around the rectangle that formed the temple's base. The columns held up the horizontal beams supporting the roof.

The Parthenon was built in the fifth century BC. It has long been considered the finest example of Greek architecture.

Carvings adorned the Parthenon inside and out. The extra care taken to make the inside impressive was rather unusual in Greek architecture. It marked a shift that would become very important to the Romans.

VOCABULARY

represent (REP ri ZENT) *v.* speak on behalf of someone; be a symbol that stands for something

distinct (dis TINGKT) *adj.* separate and different

impress (im PRES) *v.* make someone feel admiration and respect; make clear the importance of something

appreciate (uh PREE shee AYT) *v.* be grateful for; recognize worth of something or someone

The Saint Louis Art Museum in Missouri was built
using Roman style architecture.

Roman Public Buildings Roman society was focused on large gatherings. Big buildings were needed in which people could come together for worship, sports, and other types of entertainment. For this reason, architects began to **highlight** the insides of buildings as much as the outsides. One way to do this was to make the spaces bigger, especially so that the eyes were drawn upward. Roman builders used stone and brick in **innovative** ways to make arches and vaults that supported much higher roofs.

One reason the Romans could **achieve** new heights in building was because they discovered concrete. It was different from modern concrete, but it still set very hard. As a result, it was stable. As Roman buildings became bigger and taller, concrete could bear the extra weight.

Roman Arches An arch is made from wedge-shaped stones. The narrow ends point toward the inside of the arch. Arches can support heavy roofs. When arches are built in a row, they form a vault. Roman builders roofed large areas by using these tunnel vaults supported by huge pillars.

Roman builders then saw how to **reinforce** the strength of a vault by crisscrossing two arches. Once this design was mastered, the next step was the building of beautiful domes.

Vocabulary

highlight (HY lyt) *v.* draw attention to something

innovative (IN uh vayt iv) *adj.* new, different, and better

achieve (uh CHEEV) *v.* succeed in doing something; accomplish; gain

reinforce (REE in FOHRS) *v.* make stronger; support

The Pantheon The Pantheon was built in Rome in the 120s. It is the most **exquisite** example of a dome from that time. The dome soars 143 feet in height and is exactly that wide. To hold up this huge dome, the walls are 20 feet thick at their base.

The Pantheon represents the level of attention architects of the time gave to the insides of buildings. Wonderful carvings **emphasize** the beauty of the dome. Stars and an actual opening in the dome's top draw visitors' eyes and minds up toward heaven.

When we compare the Pantheon to the Parthenon, we must notice another **profound** shift in focus. Where once straight lines and perfect rectangles defined beauty, Roman arches, vaults, and domes created lovely curves. The eye now looked for a **swerve** rather than a perfect corner in seeking beauty.

The Hagia Sophia Four hundred years after the Romans built the Pantheon, an even more magnificent dome was raised in Istanbul. Around 532, construction began on the Hagia Sophia ("the Holy Wisdom"). It would **embody** the best ideas of Greek and Roman builders. This huge church was also built to suit its purpose. Architects thought carefully about the details of the worship services to be held there. They understood that the beautiful dome would stand for heaven and should feature light.

The result was a design that started with a large square. This square was divided into three rectangles. In the central rectangle, architects marked off a smaller square. They would top this area with a huge round dome. Architects designed the dome with windows in

The Hagia Sophia was built between 532 and 537 at the orders of Emperor Justinian. It is considered to be one of the most beautiful buildings in the world.

its base to let in light. The inside of the dome was covered with gold mosaics so that the whole space shimmers in the light. Today, visitors still **react** with awe to the dome's heavenly beauty.

Vocabulary

exquisite (EKS kwiz it) *adj.* beautiful in a delicate way

emphasize (EM fuh syz) *v.* stress something in order to make it stand out

profound (proh FOWND) *adj.* deeply or intensely felt

swerve (SWERV) *n.* curving motion

embody (em BAHD ee) *v.* represent an idea or quality

react (ree AKT) *v.* behave in a particular way in response to someone or something

The construction of Notre Dame Cathedral was supported and encouraged by France's King Louis VII.

Buildings Soar Higher: Gothic Architecture

Light and height continued to be features that architects emphasized for several hundred years. These two features would be best joined in the Gothic style. The Gothic period of architecture lasted from around 1150 to 1550.

As always, this new style was developed to meet new demands. People wanted light in their places of worship, but they also wanted color. Huge stained glass windows were the answer. But how could walls of glass be supported?

People also wanted bigger spaces with a good flow of air through them. Rulers held the **attitude** that the buildings should not only be bigger but more beautifully elaborate, showing great wealth. This was asking a lot. How could buildings be massive, full of glass, and also look stunningly beautiful on the outside?

Architects, working hard to solve these problems, found the answer. It was a new architectural feature called the buttress. Buttresses are huge arches that resemble curved bones. They help support the weight of soaring arches and vaults.

Notre Dame Cathedral Notre Dame was built in Paris between 1163 and 1250. Flying buttresses, half arches of stone on the outside of the building, carried the weight and pressure of the building away from the walls to huge pillars. That meant the walls could feature plenty of tall stained glass windows. The huge stained glass windows were themselves supported by delicate stone supports traced with intricate designs.

Gothic architecture combined lines and curves to create an overall effect of **supple** movement. The lines were thin and often ended in curves leading to pointed arches. Just as the master architects had planned, the design of these places of worship seemed always to point upward, toward heaven.

Vocabulary

attitude (AT uh tood) *n.* opinions or feelings, positive or negative, about something or someone

supple (SUP uhl) *adj.* able to bend easily; flexible

Modern Architecture

The great ancient and medieval architectural achievements continue to **contribute** to the success of modern building efforts. For example, domes play an important role in many public buildings in the United States. New building materials and changing ideas of beauty make modern domes unique. Yet modern architects **benefit** from the work done hundreds of years ago to create the first domes.

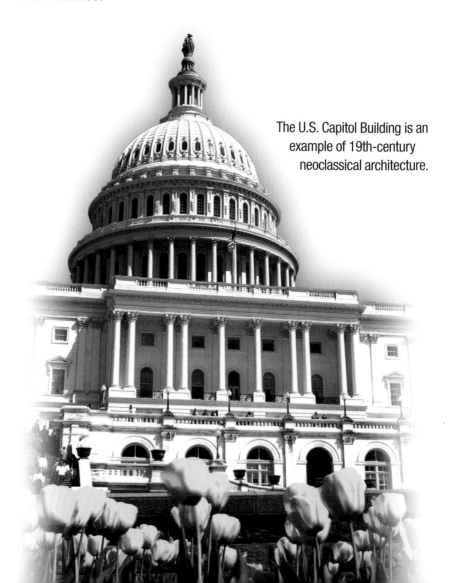

The U.S. Capitol Building is an example of 19th-century neoclassical architecture.

The U.S. Capitol George Washington knew that a dome had come to symbolize power. Therefore, he **concluded** that the only proper design for the young nation's Capitol building must include a dome.

By the time the current dome was built (1856–1863), builders were using cast iron. Cast iron was fireproof, cheaper than stone, and could create the same look found in the famous domes of the past. So, the U.S. Capitol has a dome formed mostly from iron and cables. A beautiful inner dome hid the iron ribs holding up the outer dome. It was put in place as the artist finished each piece of it.

The Astrodome The openness of domed buildings is one thing that makes them so desirable. Domes need no columns to support them. In 1965, this fact clicked in the mind of the owner of the Houston Astros. He wanted fans to be comfortable while watching his baseball team play. In muggy Texas, this meant his fans needed air conditioning. However, he didn't want columns to block their view of the game. Wouldn't a huge air-conditioned dome be the answer? It would indeed, and so the design of the modern "Eighth Wonder of the World" began.

VOCABULARY

contribute (kuhn TRIB yoot) *v.* give or share money, knowledge, or ideas

benefit (BEN uh fit) *v.* give or receive help

conclude (kuhn KLOOD) *v.* form an opinion based on evidence

The Astrodome was built of steel. A tough steel ring formed the outside of the dome. Below the ring were 72 steel columns that bore the weight from the dome. Thirty-seven more steel towers were placed inside the ring. The dome rested on these towers as it was constructed. Twelve wedge-shaped structures of steel were built from the center out. Once they were all completed and hooked together, the dome was lowered onto the steel ring, and the 37 towers were removed.

Once in place, the dome was covered with skylights made from acrylic. This allowed natural light to come in. The first time "Play ball!" rang out in the Astrodome, the players stood on real grass under the dome as 50,000 fans watched in comfort.

Unfortunately, the skylights in the Astrodome made the sunlight blinding. Players could not see fly balls. So, the skylights were painted to block out the sunlight.

Without sun the grass died. The solution? Plastic grass, or Astroturf as it came to be named! This just shows how one failed idea can **promote** a whole new idea or invention.

Thirty-five years later, on March 30, 2000, the Astros left the Astrodome for a new arena. This arena features the newest development in sports buildings. Its dome is retractable—that is, it can be opened on fine days. Modern sports arenas such as this offer both air-conditioned comfort and outdoor viewing, depending on the weather.

Vocabulary

promote (pruh MOHT) *v.* encourage; contribute to the growth of; raise to a higher level or rank

The world's first domed stadium stands 18 stories tall and covers 9 ½ acres. The dome is 710 feet in diameter and the ceiling is 208 feet above the playing surface.

Fuller's dome consisted of a space frame of steel pipes enclosing 1,900 molded acrylic panels. A fire burned away the building's acrylic cover in 1976, but the steel frame remained. Today, the dome houses a museum.

The Geodesic Dome Steel and acrylic were combined to create another stunning dome in 1967. This dome was designed as the United States Pavilion for the World Expo in Montreal, Canada.

Buckminster Fuller and Shoji Sadao designed the pavilion. Fuller was known for his geodesic domes. These were made of very light steel rods. The rods were put together to form triangles. Then the whole structure was covered with thin sheets of glass or plastic.

Triangles are very stable forms for building. Fuller trusted the strength of his domes so much that he designed one that could cover all of Manhattan! This was never built, but the dome in Montreal was 200 feet high (equal to a 20-story building) and 250 feet in diameter.

Fuller's dome at Montreal did **consist** of the same basic materials used in the Astrodome. However, it did not have the problem of too much sunlight. Fuller gave his dome shading screens. These used the retractable system of later sports arenas. That is, the shades opened and closed over parts of the dome as the sun's rays shifted.

More than 11 million people passed through the dome during Expo '67. It was described as a true wonder, both inside and out.

The Experience Music Project This 140,000-square-foot museum was built in Seattle to celebrate American pop music and culture. Completed in 2000, it was designed by leading modern architect Frank Gehry. The curving, colorful parts of the building are said to resemble the smashed parts of an electric guitar. It is no surprise, then, that the man behind the project, millionaire Paul Allen, decided to **dedicate** the building to Jimi Hendrix. This rock legend sometimes shattered his guitars during concerts.

The building seems to move and change colors. The entire building, inside and out, is curvy and colorful—capturing the supple movement of music. Yet the building's shell was formed from sturdy steel ribs and concrete. These traditional materials are covered with colorful metal panels. Some are made of lightweight aluminum, which can be seen on the outside.

VOCABULARY

consist (kuhn SIST) *v.* to be made of

dedicate (DED i kayt) *v.* devote all attention and effort to someone or something

Architecture of the Future

Architects of the future may look upon Gehry's museum as another great landmark in their profession. It will stand right up there with domes and buttresses. Why?

The Experience Music Project is a museum of music history. It is located near the Space Needle. It is also by one of the two stops on the Seattle Center Monorail, which runs through the building.

The answer is that the complex mathematics behind its design could not have been done without computer programs. Computer-generated design, like important architectural advances in the past, will surely **establish** itself as a key force in all future architecture.

Discussion Questions

1. As you examine the photos of buildings included in this article, which one do you respond to the most positively? What is it about this building that "takes your breath away" when you look at it? How does knowing more about what went into the building of it affect your reaction to it?

2. Think about the big advances humans have made in modern times, in areas such as transportation, communication, and technology. What types of new buildings have these advances required? What kinds of problems and solutions do you think architects have faced and **overcome** in designing these buildings?

3. How do you think architects might respond to what is going on in the world at the current time? How might their designs show trends in human thought and action?

VOCABULARY

establish (uh STAB lish) *v.* determine; make sure of; set up

overcome (oh vuhr KUM) *v.* successfully deal with problem that prevents you from achieving something

CHALLENGING
Assumptions

By Eoghan Stafford

*"To count is modern practice.
The ancient method was to guess."
–Samuel Johnson*

How do we respond to the world? If we want to shape and improve the world, we need to have an accurate picture of the way the world really is. Only then can we predict the **consequences** of our actions. Statistics, the study of the likelihood that something will **occur**, can help us **unravel** the causes within certain patterns. That helps us make better predictions: Will I succeed in college? Are girls better than boys in math? Will a product with funny ads sell better than a product with serious ads? Studying statistics also demonstrates the dangers of drawing false conclusions about what we see in the world around us.

VOCABULARY

consequences (KAHN suh kwens iz) *n.* results of an action

occur (uh KER) *v.* happen; take place

unravel (un RAV uhl) *v.* become untangled or separated

Firefighters, EMTs, and police officers are there to respond in the likelihood that we need their help.

Someday these students will be attending college. Statistics can help predict how successful they will be in college.

What Is Statistics?

Statistics is a branch of mathematics. It involves **interpreting** numerical data taken from the real world. People use statistics to make **generalizations**— or inferences—about a specific population. A *population* is a group of things that a person wants to study. It could **consist** of people—such as students, families, or voters— or things—like cities, cougars in a national park, or best-selling books. Statistical inferences are based on a sample drawn from a population. A *sample* is a small part of a larger population. Not just any sample will do, however. To make accurate inferences about a population, a person must use a typical portion of the larger population. This is called a *representative* sample.

Why Do We Need Statistics?

Statistics can help us make better predictions about what to expect in life. Let's consider an example. Some people say that students who succeed in high-school classes and SAT tests are more likely to succeed in college than students who are less successful in these areas. Others say that students' performance in high-school classes and on the SAT test has nothing to do with college achievement. Who is right?

One study used statistics to answer this question. The researchers used a sample of about 53,000 students who entered college in 1985. The data they collected were the students' high school GPAs, SAT scores, and whether or not they had graduated college in 1989. **Refer** to the table on the next page, which summarizes their data.

VOCABULARY

interpret (in TER pruht) *v.* to explain the meaning of something; translate

generalization (jen uhr uhl i ZAY shuhn) *n.* a statement that may be true in some or many situations but is not true all of the time

consist (kuhn SIST) *v.* to be made of

refer (ri FER) *v.* consult a source to find information; mention a source of information

Each column (top to bottom) shows the college graduation rates of students who had the same SAT score but different GPAs. Each row (left to right) shows the graduation rates of students with the same GPA but different SAT scores. The cells where a row and column cross tell us the graduation rate for all the students with that GPA and SAT score. For example, look at the cell in the second row from the top and the third column from the right. It tells us that 58% of students with an A– average and an SAT score between 1000 and 1149 graduated college in four years.

College Graduation Rates
by High School GPA and SAT Score

GPA	SAT Score					
	Less than 700	700–849	850–999	1000–1149	1150–1299	1300 or higher
A, A+	28%	45%	55%	64%	71%	80%
A–	29%	41%	52%	58%	65%	73%
B+	29%	38%	46%	56%	62%	63%
B	21%	32%	39%	46%	51%	48%
B–	17%	26%	33%	35%	44%	38%
C+	17%	18%	24%	27%	28%	—
Less than C+	10%	16%	19%	21%	—	—

The symbol "—" indicates cases where there was not enough data.
GPA = Grade Point Average
SAT = Scholastic Aptitude Test

What did the researchers find? In each of the rows, going from left to right, the graduation rate gets higher. This means that students with higher SAT scores were more likely to graduate college in four years. In the columns, going from bottom to top, the graduation rate gets higher. This means that students with higher grades in high school were more likely to graduate college in four years. Thus, statistics demonstrates that success in high school is related to success in college. We can predict that students with higher grades and test scores will do better in college by a **considerable** degree.

Statistics can provide the **benefit** of clear answers to many important questions. Do public service ads make passengers more likely to wear a seat belt? Do people who speak two languages earn higher salaries? Will students learn more if class sizes are reduced? These are questions that statistics can help answer.

A Statistical Puzzle

By using statistics we often find that things aren't quite what they seem. Imagine two basketball players, Huffman and Bedford. In a particular season, Huffman outshoots Bedford in both two-point and three-point shots. Yet, according to the percentages, Bedford outshoots Huffman overall. How can this be?

VOCABULARY

indicate (IN di kayt) *v.* point out; show

considerable (kuhn SID er uh buhl) *adj.* large enough to be important; worth noting

benefit (BEN uh fit) *n.* a gain or positive result

The table below **displays** the shots each player attempted during the season. The "2-Point Shots" column gives the number of attempts each player made from the two-point range, the number of their successful shots, and success rates (the number of successful shots divided by the number of shots they attempted). The "3-Point Shots" column gives the same information for shots they made from the three-point range. In the two-point category, Huffman made 44.9% of the shots he attempted. Bedford only made 43.3% of his attempts. In the three-point category, Huffman made 35% of the shots he attempted, while Bedford made 0%.

Huffman and Bedford's Season Stats

	2-Point Shots	3-Point Shots	Total
Bedford's Attempts	30	1	31
Bedford's Successful Shots	13	0	13
Bedford's Success Rate	43.3%	0%	41.9%
Huffman's Attempts	127	100	227
Huffman's Successful Shots	57	35	92
Huffman's Success Rate	44.9%	35%	40.5%

The "Total" column gives the total number of shots they attempted (both two-point and three-point shots), the total number they made successfully, and their overall success rates for the season. Even though Huffman performed better in each category, for the whole season, Bedford made 41.9% of the shots he attempted. Huffman made slightly less: 40.5%. So we might think Bedford is the better player.

One basketball player successfully blocks the two-point shot of his opponent.

However, this ignores how hard it is to make each shot. Three-point shots are clearly harder to make than two-point shots. Only one out of Bedford's thirty-one attempts was from the three-point range. That's about 3% of his attempts. Huffman made about 44% of his attempted shots from the three-point range. We can't make an accurate comparison of Bedford and Huffman's abilities until we consider how hard each shot was. At this point, if Bedford **challenged** Huffman to a game, whom would you predict to win?

Simpson's Paradox

The Bedford/Huffman situation is an example of some-thing called Simpson's Paradox. The paradox refers to a strange thing that can occur when you divide a set of data into several smaller sections. Sometimes a pattern that appears in a very small section of the data does not appear when you look at all the data together. In fact, you may even find the opposite pattern when you look at the whole set of data.

Simpson's Paradox shows that it is easy to draw false conclusions if you don't look at the data in context. It is important to consider other explanations for patterns besides the obvious ones. In this example, it appeared at first that Huffman is a worse player than Bedford. Yet this was a false conclusion. It turns out Huffman just at-tempts difficult shots more often than Bedford.

Correlation and Causation

Another error people often make is to assume that if two things happen at the same time, one thing must be making the other thing happen. When people make this mistake they are confusing correlation with causation. A *correlation* is an association between two things. For instance, eating a lot of greasy food is correlated with being overweight. The two things tend to go together. Similarly, seeing earthworms on the sidewalks can be correlated with seeing people carrying umbrellas.

Causation means that one thing has *made* another thing happen. Eating too much greasy food ***causes*** people to gain weight. Earthworms on the sidewalk don't *cause* people to carry umbrellas. It is the rain that causes both earthworms to come up out of the ground and people to carry umbrellas. When we see a correlation between two things, it doesn't always mean that one thing caused the other.

VOCABULARY

causes (KAWZ uhz) *v.* makes something happen; results in

Falling rain causes these people to put up their umbrellas.

The Mozart Effect

Consider the so-called "Mozart effect." Some studies have found that high school students who enroll in music classes tend to have higher test scores in English and math than students who choose not to take music classes. Some people view this as evidence that listening to music makes young people smarter. In fact, the state of Georgia used to give Mozart CDs to families to play for their babies!

These studies confuse correlation and causation, as more thoughtful researchers have **emphasized**. Just because taking music classes is *correlated* with

high performance in English and math doesn't mean that studying music *causes* students to do better in other classes. It could be that students who do well in English and math classes just enjoy learning. Thus, they are more likely to take music electives.

Listening to music does not cause young people to become smarter. However, there is a correlation between taking music electives and enjoying learning.

Experiments and Causation

So how can we **establish** if one thing is actually causing another? One way is to conduct an experiment. Participants in an experiment are randomly chosen to receive or not receive a treatment. The first group is called the *treatment* group. The second group is called the *control* group. For example, to test whether caffeine **affects** the amount of sleep people get, an experimenter would have the treatment group drink a caffeinated drink like tea or coffee. They would *not* give the drink to the control group. The experimenter would then measure how many hours of sleep each group got the next night. Let's say the treatment group got much less sleep than the control group. The experimenter could then reasonably **conclude** that the caffeine had *caused* members of the treatment group to sleep less.

Sample Bias

We're calling to ask if you have a telephone . . .

We can also be misled if a sample is not representative of the population from which it is drawn. In 1936, a poll was taken asking people which candidate in the upcoming presidential election they were going to vote for: Alfred M. Landon or Franklin D. Roosevelt. The people taking the poll used phone books to pick a few hundred people from around the country. They called these people to ask who they were voting for. The polltakers found that most of their sample planned to vote for Landon. Yet, Roosevelt won the election in a landslide!

"We're calling to ask if you have a telephone . . ."

A sample bias—the method used in taking the poll—resulted in a wrong conclusion. Franklin Roosevelt (bottom) beat Alfred Landon (top) in the 1936 presidential election.

VOCABULARY

establish (uh STAB lish) *v.* determine; make sure of; set up

affect (uh FEKT) *v.* produce a change in or have an influence over something or someone

conclude (kuhn KLOOD) *v.* form an opinion based on evidence

It turned out that the sample did not **represent** the whole population of American voters very well. You see, in 1936, during the Great Depression, people who had phones tended to have more money than people who didn't have phones. And wealthier people tended to support Landon's platform rather than Roosevelt's.

This story **highlights** the problems caused by sample bias. Sample bias means taking a sample of a population that is not representative of that population. Let us **restate** what was said earlier. We *can only make judgments about a population if our sample is representative of that population.*

Now let's **elaborate** on what it means for a sample to be representative. If you want to create a representative sample, you have to pick a random selection from the population you are studying. No member of the population should be more likely to be chosen than any other. Because a random sample consists of observations chosen this way, the sample is typical of the whole population being studied.

The Perils of Overgeneralizing

Even if a sample is representative, you can't always **infer** that what is true of that population is true of another, or even the same population at a different time. Correlations can change from place to place and from time to time.

Economists have tried to identify the factors that cause some countries to be rich and some to be poor. One pattern they have noted is that countries close to the equator tend to have less income than countries in the temperate zones. Yet this correlation is not

The correlation between countries' wealth and their climate has changed over time. It will probably change again.

carved in stone. Five hundred years ago, it was the societies in the tropics that were wealthier. By looking at more data—in this case, data from both the past and the present—economists learned that the relationship between countries' climate and their wealth has changed. This correlation could change again in the future. Today, countries like India and Botswana that used to be poor are currently developing higher standards of living.

VOCABULARY

represent (REP ri ZENT) *v.* speak on behalf of someone; be a symbol that stands for something

highlight (HY lyt) *v.* draw attention to something

restate (ree STAYT) *v.* say something again; summarize

elaborate (ee LAB uh RAYT) *v.* expand with details

infer (in FER) *v.* make a logical assumption based on evidence or reasoning

Conclusion

Statistics shows that our first impressions about the world are often incorrect. In spite of a few cautions, such as sample bias, statistics are very useful. They give us the data we need to respond with understanding to the patterns and events we see in our world. By gathering more information and considering all possible explanations for the patterns we find, we can **enrich** our understanding of the world and shape it more effectively.

Tools to gather information have improved since these materials were used in the 1930s. However, we still must use caution in gathering and interpreting the patterns we see in our world.

Discussion Questions

1. Imagine that an expert on television says that having more police on the street causes crime rates to go up. When the interviewer **communicates** surprise, the expert refers to a chart showing that cities with more police officers tend to have higher crime rates. Is the expert's evidence convincing? Why or why not? What might be a different explanation for the pattern in the expert's chart?

2. Suppose you wanted to convince your principal that allowing students to start and end the school day an hour later would improve their academic performance. Describe how you could demonstrate this using one of the methods discussed in this article.

3. The owner of an auto repair shop tells you: "Most of the teenagers who come to my repair shop are very careless drivers. That's how I know that most teenagers are reckless drivers." Why is the shop owner's reasoning an example of sample bias? What other generalizations about teenagers are examples of sample bias?

4. "Correlation does not equal causation." What does this mean? See if you can **paraphrase** this statement in your own words.

VOCABULARY

enrich (en RICH) *v.* give more value or effectiveness to

communicate (kuh MYOO ni kayt) *v.* to make ideas or feelings known

paraphrase (PAR uh FRAYZ) *v.* restate something in your own words

Glossary

achieve (uh CHEEV) *v.* succeed in doing something; accomplish; gain **19, 45**

affect (uh FEKT) *v.* produce a change in or have an influence over something or someone **19, 70**

appreciate (uh PREE shee AYT) *v.* be grateful for; recognize worth of something or someone **38, 42**

attitude (AT uh tood) *n.* opinions or feelings, positive or negative, about something or someone **35, 49**

benefit (BEN uh fit) *n.* gain; positive result **10, 63**

benefit (BEN uh fit) *v.* give or receive help **38, 50**

brawny (BRAWN ee) *adj.* strong and muscular **5**

causes (KAWZ uhz) *v.* makes something happen; results in **66**

challenge (CHAL uhnj) *v.* call to take part in a contest or competition **28, 65**

communicate (kuh MYOO ni kayt) *v.* to make ideas or feelings known **30, 75**

conclude (kuhn KLOOD) *v.* form an opinion based on evidence **6, 51, 70**

consequences (KAHN suh kwens iz) *n.* results of an action **59**

considerable (kuhn SID er uh buhl) *adj.* large enough to be important; worth noting **6, 34, 63**

consist (kuhn SIST) *v.* to be made of **24, 55, 60**

contribute (kuhn TRIB yoot) *v.* give or share money, knowledge, or ideas **39, 50**

cooperate (koh AHP er AYT) *v.* work together with others for a common purpose **37**

curious (KYOOR ee uhs) *adj.* eager to learn or know **23**

dedicate (DED i kayt) *v.* devote all attention and effort to someone or something **55**

detect (dee TEKT) *v.* notice or discover something **28**

dislodge (dis LAHJ) *v.* force from a position or place **23**

display (di SPLAY) *v.* exhibit objects or feelings so they can be seen easily **26, 64**

distinct (dis TINGKT) *adj.* separate and different **16, 42**

elaborate (ee LAB uh RAYT) *v.* expand with details **72**

embody (em BAHD ee) *v.* represent an idea or quality **46**

emphasize (EM fuh syz) *v.* stress something in order to make it stand out **46, 68**

engaged (en GAYJD) *v.* entered into conflict with **12**

enrich (en RICH) *v.* give more value or effectiveness to **8, 74**

establish (uh STAB lish) *v.* determine; make sure of; set up **9, 57, 70**

expel (ex SPEL) *v.* drive out by force; eject; dismiss **15**

exquisite (EKS kwiz it) *adj.* beautiful in a delicate way **46**

generalization (jen uhr uhl i ZAY shuhn) *n.* a statement that may be true in some or many situations but is not true all of the time **60**

generate (JEN er ayt) *v.* produce or create something **16**

highlight (HY lyt) *v.* draw attention to something **45, 72**

impress (im PRES) *v.* make someone feel admiration and respect; make clear the importance of something **42**

incessantly (in SES uhnt lee) *adv.* without stopping **30**

indicate (IN di kayt) *v.* point out; show **62**

infer (in FER) *v.* make a logical assumption based on evidence or reasoning **24, 72**

innovative (IN uh vayt iv) *adj.* new, different, and better **45**

interpret (in TER pruht) *v.* to explain the meaning of something; translate **60**

isolated (EYE suh layt uhd) *adj.* set apart **4**

loathed (LOHTHD) *v.* hated **8**

luminous (LOO muh nuhs) *adj.* giving off light **15, 29**

occur (uh KER) *v.* happen; take place **12, 29, 59**

overcome (oh vuhr KUM) *v.* successfully deal with problem that prevents you from achieving something **57**

paraphrase (PAR uh FRAYZ) *v.* restate something in your own words **75**

passage (PAS ij) *n.* a section of writing **12**

profound (proh FOWND) *adj.* deeply or intensely felt **6, 46**

promote (pruh MOHT) *v.* encourage; contribute to the growth of; raise to a higher level or rank **53**

protects (proh TEKTS) *v.* shields from injury, danger, or loss; guards; defends **5**

react (ree AKT) *v.* behave in a particular way in response to someone or something **8, 47**

refer (ri FER) *v.* consult a source to find information; mention a source of information **61**

reinforce (REE in FOHRS) *v.* make stronger; support **33, 45**

represent (REP ri ZENT) *v.* speak on behalf of someone; be a symbol that stands for something **6, 42, 72**

restate (ree STAYT) *v.* say something again; summarize **72**

risky (ris KEE) *adj.* hazardous; dangerous **39**

strive (STRYV) *v.* struggle; work hard **7**

supple (SUP uhl) *adj.* able to bend easily; flexible **49**

swerve (SWERV) *n.* curving motion **46**

torrent (TOHR uhnt) *n.* flood; rush **36**

transfixed (tranz FIKST) *adj.* rooted to or focused on a spot **23**

transform (trans FOHRM) *v.* change the shape or structure of something or someone **6, 36**

unravel (un RAV uhl) *v.* become untangled or separated **59**

utter (UT er) *v.* speak **5**

Photo Credits